OUR CONDO ON WHEELS

Story of a couple RVing

Diane Lenamon

AuthorHouse™
1663 Liberty Drive
Bloomington, IN 47403
www.authorhouse.com
Phone: 1 (800) 839-8640

Published by AuthorHouse 06/15/2020

ISBN: 978-1-7283-6035-5 (sc)
ISBN: 978-1-7283-6034-8 (e)

Library of Congress Control Number: 2020907756

THIS PAGE IS DEDICATED WITH THANKS AND LOVE
TO MY HUSBAND WALTER LENAMON WHO HAS SEEN
ME THROUGH SO MUCH AND BEEN THERE FOR ME.
I WOULD LIKE TO THANK SUSAN MOSES FOR
EDITING MY BOOK. SHE HAD BEEN SO GRACE'S
IN DOING SO. THANK YOU AGAIN.

Chapter 1

• • • • • •

The day is finally here; I'm to leave on an afternoon flight to California. I have four days off and I'm going to see my two grandsons and son-in-law. I arrived late afternoon and all three were there to meet me. On the way to their home, we stopped and had dinner. We had such a good visit, and continued with our visit when we arrived at their home. We sat up and talked and later watched a movie. I retired later. It had been a long day. When I awoke, I went out by the pool and just said a long prayer, how grateful I was to be able to come and that everyone was in good health. The boys finally got up and I asked what they might like to do for the next couple of days. Ken said he would like to go to Yosemite National Park, Keith wanted to play golf with Granny (that's me). I told the boys to get dressed, we would get some breakfast on the way to Yosemite and would play golf the next day.

The oldest grandson, Ken, said his car would never make it to Yosemite. Could we rent a car? I asked him if it would make it to Fresno where my flight came in, and he said he thought so. We started our little trip, picked up a rental car at the airport and continued to Yosemite. We had a wonderful time together and saw a lot of wildlife around the visitors center, there were so many chipmunks. The boys went in the center and got some peanuts to feed them while I took pictures. Late in the afternoon we started back to their home, but before that we took the rental car back to the airport. We got back to their place and just collapsed. It was a very enjoyable day. The next day we got up and got ready to play golf. I told the boys I hoped they had rental clubs and shoes for I didn't bring any.

They said their dad would have what I needed, for he worked at the pro shop. We arrived at the country club and I found everything I needed. We played nine holes, ate lunch, and then back out for the next nine holes. Ken and Keith said they really enjoyed playing with their Granny.

After we got back to their home, I asked Keith and Ken what they would like for dinner. They both said, please fix a roast that you make so well. Well while the boys were getting their homework, I went to the store in my grandson's car, not knowing if I would make it or not. I got all the shopping done and returned to prepare the roast and other things for dinner. Ken asked to invite his girlfriend over for dinner; he said he wanted me to meet her. I said it was fine with me if his dad said it was alright. He did and dinner went well, even the boys' dad enjoyed everything. I surprised them with a chocolate cake I picked up at the bakery, and they all thought that was wonderful.

I had to leave the next day, so after finishing dinner I went to pack and get ready for my flight home. It was such a happy time with everyone. Mark, my son-in-law, wanted to know if he could help in any way, and I suggested he set the alarm for the next morning. I had a very early flight to make. It seemed that the alarm went off before I even closed my eyes; I guess I was a little tired, slept like a baby. I got dressed gave Ken and Keith a hug and kiss, off to school they went.

My son-in-law took me to the airport, but before we got started to Fresno, which was about forty-five miles from where we were, Mark had to stop and get gas. We went back into town from his house, which is a longer distance then what we should have done. I became very antsy for I was getting short of time for my flight. I asked my son-in-law to please hurry, then he went back in the store and came out with some coffee for us. I really appreciated that, but I was losing a lot of time.

We finally got on the road and got to Fresno with just a short time before my plane was to take off. Then of all things Mark said he forgot what exit to take, by then I was beside myself for I had taken a different route when I went to get the rental car. I looked to my right, and said, "there is an airplane taking off, turn right." Thank goodness, we went right in front of the terminal. I got out trying to get my one piece of luggage, when Mark wanted to take it to the plane for me. I just gave him a hug, thanked him for everything and took off. I got to the boarding area and they were just getting ready to close the door for the plane to depart. I said, "please wait, I need to board." The attendant said, "You sure are lucky, another second and we would not be able to let you on board."

Chapter 2

・・・●・・・

As I was going down the aisle to my seat, I was looking at the aisle numbers and realized someone sitting in my seat. When I approached my seat, a gentleman was sitting there, and I told him he was in the wrong seat. He said no, the flight attendant told him to sit there. I had my ticket in my hand and showed him that it was my seat the flight attendant came and asked if there was a problem. I told her yes and went over the whole issue again. She looked at the gentleman's ticket and it was a seat across the aisle, so he got up and moved.

Well I finally got settled in my seat and pulled out my book to read and this gentleman stated talking to me, so I couldn't read any of my book on the flight. It went on the entire flight to the Dallas/Fort Worth airport. When we got ready to land, he asked me if he could call me sometime, for he had a daughter that lived in the Fort Worth area. I truly felt like a pick-up so I gave him one of my business cards and told him to call me at the office for I was there more than I was at home. He said he had another trip to take but would get with me as soon as he returned home. The plane landed, we both left the plane, he had to take another flight home from DFW. My daughter was scheduled to pick me up and take me home. I'll always remember this trip. The doors were opening for a new life.

Several days later, I get this post card in the mail at work from Branson, Missouri. Well the guys I worked for, who are engineers, had already read it and asked me, "what are you doing being picked up on the plane?" I kindly told them it was none of their business, but I have to say they were very protective of me, since I had lost my first husband. I told them about the gentleman I had met, and I had given him my business card, not my home number. I got them all convinced, and they said no more about it.

The next week I got a call at my office from this gentleman (Maurice). He asked me to go to lunch, for he was in town visiting his daughter. I asked him where he wanted to go, and he said I'll pick you up at your office. I told him I could meet him, but he insisted. I told him where I worked and how to get there. I told one of the engineers to take down his license plate number when we drove off, which he did. I guess being a widow I was too protective of myself, which I felt was a good thing. We had a very nice lunch, and a lot of conversation. I believe we learned a lot about each other in that one hour. Over several weeks we saw each other quite often and really enjoyed one another. He would come to Fort Worth and visit, or I would go to Horseshoe Bay to his place. We were always going somewhere on the weekend. I found out he really liked to travel, and I did also. I had told him that when I retire, I was planning on traveling, not knowing that it was really in my future.

I went to spend the weekend with him and that is when I met his daughter and family. I was so glad to meet everyone, and just feel things out somewhat. They all made me feel very welcome. Did I say that when Maurice and I met it was the week before 9-11. That day I will never forget, where I was, what I was doing. The reason Maurice won me over was that he was in Branson when he called to see if I was alright and where I was, or where I was going. I told him that they told everyone in the office to leave and go home, until further notice. I immediately left and went by the grocery store to get some things I was needing, then went home. I turned on the television and stayed glued to it. I returned to work several days later. Our minds were not on our work, but we worked through it everyone else during those terrible days.

Chapter 3

A week before Christmas, my children and I had our Christmas at my house. We always shared taking turns each year. We always had Christmas a week early so the grandchildren could be home for Christmas. I asked the children if they minded if I invited Maurice, and they were all for it. They were anxious to meet him, and they all really enjoyed him being there. We had a lot of quality time and took a lot of pictures.

Just after Thanksgiving that year, Maurice had called me to go with him and his youngest daughter and grandsons to the Christmas parade at downtown Fort Worth. They came by and I got to meet his number two daughter and family for the first time. She was expecting her third child then. We arrived downtown, got our chairs out and found a good place to sit. It was so cold, but we enjoyed the parade very much. So now I have met both of his daughters. I thought to myself, "where is this going?"

After the New Year, Maurice came into town, and I fixed dinner for us. After dinner we went out on the patio, and I told him some more about my family and he wanted to know why I lived in such a large place. Well, first it's near to my very close friend that I've known for a very long time. Second, I had really gotten the townhouse for my middle daughter and me to live in, but that just didn't work out. I continued to stay there as it was also close to my work. He wanted to know what I thought about traveling. I thought to myself, "what's he leading up to?" I expressed myself about what I wanted to do after retiring, but knew it wasn't going to be any time soon.

I just didn't know what God had planned for me. He asked me to come to Horseshoe Bay the next weekend. He wanted to show me something. All along he had been researching about motorhomes. I arrived at his place on Friday evening. He had dinner ready, and it was so refreshing that we didn't go out and eat. He's a very good cook, that's a plus. The next morning he said, "let's take a little ride." We started our day going to Boerne, Texas, to look at some motorhomes. We looked at so many it was mind boggling. This was a new experience for me. We started back to his place and stopped on the way for a bite to eat. He asked me what I thought about the coaches we had looked at. I expressed myself the best way I could, not knowing what I was really talking about. When we got back to his house, he asked me when I planned to retire. I said retire, I haven't thought about it really, probably in a few years. I asked him what he was thinking about. He said he had been all over the world traveling when he was working, and he wanted to travel by motor coach. I asked, what is that to do with me. Well he said I would like for you to go with me. Boy was my mind spinning, I could hardly speak. The next morning when I got up, he was already in the kitchen cooking breakfast, boy was this a surprise, I'll take this any day. After a very nice breakfast, we went out on the patio to talk more about yesterday. I told him I would contact human resources about my retirement and let him know.

Later in the day we went riding over to a beautiful area that was full of maple leaves and hills. The hill country is so magnificent, especially in the fall with all the colors of flowers and trees. The one thing I noticed about Maurice is that he is so comfortable to be with. He's such a gentleman. I thought to myself, God's knows what he's doing that was a blessing for me.

The next day I left to go home, which was a four-hour drive for me, and I thought I could really do some thinking going home. I turned out to be a beautiful cool day, so I opened my sunroof and enjoyed the drive home. I couldn't get it out of my head the things we had talked about, like traveling, retiring. It all sounded so wonderful, but could I really do this now? I arrived home, got settled, and called Maurice to let him know I had gotten home. He said not to forget about what we had talked about. I assured him I thought about it all the way home.

Monday when I got to work and everything kind of settled down, I called Human Resources and asked about my retirement, which they were totally in disbelief. "What do you mean you want to retire?" I told them I was just inquiring, that's all. The person I talked with, who I knew well, said she would send me all the information on retiring. I thanked her and hung up the phone, hoping it wouldn't go any further than between her and me. That evening I called Maurice and told him all about the phone call, which he was very happy to hear. We talked some more about traveling and told him I would see him that weekend. Maurice was coming up for the weekend to see his daughter and family.

My birthday was coming up and you will never guess what happened, Maurice had ordered a motor coach and it had come in on my birthday, Feb 1. He had never driven a motor coach for a long distance, but he picked it up in Dallas and drove to Fort Worth, stopping by his daughter's house. When I got off work, I met him at an RV park close to my house. The RV was beautiful and so long I was so surprised. The next day we headed for Ink's Lake. I was in the car and Maurice was driving the motor coach, which was a condo on wheels. We both got out to go in the park office to register for a space and Maurice realized the coach was locked, and the keys were in the ignition. Well, the park personnel was standing there in awe. Maurice called the motor coach office in Lewisville, and they gave him a number to call for a locksmith in the lake area. The locksmith came over and worked about forty-five minutes, but to no avail could he open the coach. Well then two park rangers appeared and checked all the windows, which we had already done, but found a window behind the driver's side unlocked, so they opened it and planned to go through the window. I told them I would rather them not go in, just help me get into the window. That was an experience I must say. I got on the back of their truck and climbed into the bed of the truck. They put their arms together like a bridge and I stood on their arms. I told the guys 'please don't drop me." I tried climbing in with my knees on the windowsill but had to come back out. I went back into the window one leg at a time and made it. Then I opened the door and Maurice got in and we were off to our assigned spot. Oh, what a time that was; parking a forty-foot motor coach. It took Maurice about twenty minutes, and we were using walkie talkies to guide him in. You try parking a forty-foot motor coach for the first time, it's a pure challenge. He finally got it parked, and really did a good job. Maurice stayed at Ink's Lake for about six weeks, and I went down each weekend to be there and learn different things about the coach. Ink's Lake is a beautiful place to be. One morning we were eating breakfast, and two little birds kept pecking at the window we were sitting by. They were little baby woodpeckers that saw themselves in the Dura pane window.

On Monday Maurice left Ink's Lake and had to take the motor coach back to Lewisville to have some service done. He thought he would be there a couple of days but ended up for a week and a half. After he got the coach back, he brought it over to Fort Worth and was there for six weeks at an RV park not far from where I lived.

Chapter 4

•••••••

March 30, 2002, I gave notice to move from the condo I lived in on April 30. I retired on the 3rd of May with six years at my job. Maurice and I started packing my belongings to store. I took a load to Maurice's house, to my youngest daughter's house, and my oldest daughter came up from Houston and got two loads. Then my neighbor, who is my very close friend, let me store a lot of things at her house, which I was very grateful to all.

My office had a great retirement party, and I received a lot of nice things. Everyone was so nice. Maurice helped make it possible for me to retire and for me to believe in myself. It's very true, "Believe in the Lord" with all your heart, and all things are possible.

My oldest daughter and her husband came on Friday the 3rd of May and visited Maurice and me at the RV park. The next day Maurice's oldest daughter, husband, and two daughters came, and we had a picnic outside by the motor-coach. My daughter and her husband came back by and met Maurice's daughter and family, which was very nice.

Sunday, Maurice and I met his youngest daughter and family at church. After church we went to his youngest daughter's home for lunch before we returned to church for Maurice's grandson to be baptized around 1:15 on the 5th of May. Maurice and I left for our six-month trip later that afternoon. It was like a dream come true. Maurice and I love to travel, and I truly feel the Lord put us together to be able to do our travels together. I'm a firm believer in living in faith.

Chapter 5

M aurice and I arrived in Midland-Odessa late that afternoon of May 5, 2002. Bad weather was moving close, so we pulled into our first Walmart parking lot to spend our first night on the road. We left Midland-Odessa the next morning headed for Monahan, Texas where we went to the Sand Hills, which are in a state park. It was awesome, you would have thought you were in the desert far away. Then we traveled on down the interstate, until we stopped at a roadside rest stop and took pictures at Texas Canyon, with all kinds of rock shapes. It looked like a piece of artwork. We left there and traveled to Las Cruces, New Mexico. After we got settled in our RV park in Las Cruces, we ventured into town for something to eat. Well, we found our-selves down in Ole Town that was celebrating an election for a new governor of New Mexico (the place in Historic Old Mesilla). They were also celebrating Cinco de Mayo.

Our next day we traveled to Tonopah, a town just west of Phoenix, Arizona and parked at a nice RV park for the night. The next morning we got up and started for Palm Springs, California, to visit with Maurice's brother and sister-in-law. Maurice's brother was in a nursing home, we visited with him for several hours, then left and made a few phone calls and had some lunch. After finishing our lunch we went back in the motor coach and headed to Redlands, CA. We left Redlands the next morning and headed into Bakersfield, CA in the early afternoon. We got the coach washed, then had a nice picnic in the city park. After lunch we got settled into the RV park, we were to stay in while visiting friends of Maurice's. After we visited for a while, Maurice's friends took us to their country club for dinner and met with the rest of their family. The friends were great and now very good friends of mine too.

The next day of our adventure, we left Bakersfield and traveled to see my two grandsons that I had visited when I met Maurice on the airplane. It was so good to see them again. We took them and their dad out to dinner, and we all went to the fairgrounds where the RV park was and visited for a while. They were having an FFA showing, so we walked around and looked at all the animals and said our goodbyes and returned to our coach.

On the road again, as we traveled to Fresno, CA to visit with Maurice's son and family. We arrived on Saturday and was so happy to meet his son and family. They all came out and looked the coach over inside and out. They just loved the coach, and we took pictures of everyone standing by the door of the coach. We had a god visit, then went out for dinner. The next day, Maurice and I went to church and returned to his son's house. Monday Maurice's son, Maurice and I went to Yosemite Park, took a lot of pictures and saw my first pink Dogwood flowers. Being brought up in the south, we only had white Dogwood flowers. The trees there are like giants, we walked all over the area. Later we went for lunch at the Ahwahnee Lodge, a very interesting place in Yosemite. The next day we all went to Maurice's grandson's school performance in Clovis, CA. It was so interesting to see the little ones performing. We had a great visit with the family and left on Wednesday for Redding, CA.

We arrived in Redding, CA, at a very nice, new RV park on the Sacramento River. It was so relaxing sitting by the water, also taking walks in the morning while we were there. The first time I saw a cat on a leash was in the park. I stopped and talked with the owner, and she said long as you start when they are small it's not hard to train a cat to walk with a leash. That was amazing to me.

We had several outings while we were in Redding, including Shasta Lake. The city of Shasta is a real nice place, they have a ski resort there.

Burney, CA is an old logging town, we went to the museum. We spent one night in Diamond Lake, a beautiful park, full of chipmunks everywhere. They had just opened for the summer season. We also went to Crater Lake, it is unbelievable. The lake is 1900 feet deep, a real deep blue. We did a lot of walking and picture taking. They say the lake is full of Indian spirits.

Chapter 6

· · ● · ·

Well I hope I haven't bored you yet, plenty of travels to go.in the book I will be showing all kinds of pictures that we took, and hope you enjoy them.

Junction City, Oregon, is where the factory is located that manufactured our coach. They have free parking for each customer (free in a scene if you know what I mean). Junction City is not far from Eugene, Oregon, which is a large city. When we got all set up with the coach, we walked around town then came back and just relaxed and met some more people that were there getting their coach serviced. A couple of days later we went through the factory that is the maker of our coach and learned an awful lot. We were very impressed. The next day my sister and brother-in-law arrived, and we were together for two weeks. Maurice and I took a ride over to the Oregon coast and walked around Ole-Town and had lunch. We traveled up Hwy 1 and looked at different areas. I believe the Oregon coastline is one of the most beautiful coastlines in the U.S.

My sister and brother-in-law went with us the next day to the Oregon Gardens, and they were breathtaking. We took long walks through the garden and took so many pictures. On the way back to Junction City we stopped at a real nice fruit and vegetable store and loaded up. I don't think I've ever eaten so many fresh picked cherries.

The next day we went into Eugene, Oregon, with my sister and her husband to do some shopping and have a picnic in the park there. We also went to the city market and a mall. There were so many stores to go to, we didn't cover half of them. That evening my sister and her husband had another couple join us for a few days traveling.

Charter 7

• • ● • •

June 1, thru July 31, 2002

All six of us went to the Saturday Market Center (outdoors) in Olympia. We had a nice time looking and shopping and brought some salmon to cook that night. Brenda, my sister and I went to visit one of our mother's old friends, Heidi. She was born and raised in Germany. She is a very interesting person and very sweet. That night we had our cook-out and all six of us fixed some extras to have.

Well, we all went to Mt. Rainier for the day. It was breathtaking. We went into the gift shop at the lodge and did some shopping. Maurice bought me a little bear made from the ashes from Mt. St. Helen. We went to the museum there also. (Oh, the air was so fresh and clear). When we started back to Olympia, we stopped at a place on the road where an artist lived. He was making things out of iron, and we took a lot of pictures there. Also took pictures of trains that were used for motels. We had a nice picnic on the way back to the RV park.

We arrived in Seattle today, and parked in the Boeing Aircraft parking lot. We took the plant and flight line tour. We went to the museum of all the history of Boeing, which was very interesting. We parked in the Walmart parking lot for the night. Before turning in for the night, we went to downtown Seattle to the top of the space needle and ate dinner, all six of us. It was a nice view on the observation deck. It was so strange to be up so high eating our dinner. We got back to Walmart and left for Whidbey Island in Washington. After getting parked and hooked up, we all went to eat Chinese food. The park in Whidbey is quite nice. We left in the morning to do some shopping and get our mail. Maurice and I went over to Burlington and did some shopping. Went to the next town to get our mail (Bellingham). He received his, mine didn't come I was little upset, but things happen for a reason. Went by the Post Office the next day on the way to Canada.

Well, the gang got together and had dinner at our coach tonight. We had great food and great send off.

We arrived in Surrey, Canada, and got all set up and relaxed a while. Went to see where you catch the ferry, for we're going to Victoria in the morning. After we found where to get the ferry, we went to White Rock, which is on the waterfront with a beach (too cold to swim). Maurice and I had a wonderful meal at Charley's in Surrey. On the way back to the RV park we got lost. What an experience.

Chapter 8

•••••••

We got up real early and got the ferry to Victoria, Island. When we arrived, went to the Butchart Garden, which was amazing. The city of Victoria is on a waterfront and is so beautiful. We went to the Empress Hotel and had high tea, House of Parliament and several churches dated back to the 1800's. After a wonderful day, we went back to ride the ferry to Surrey. Maurice said that he always wanted to take a cruise. Our first cruise was on a ferry…

Maurice and I went back to Bellingham to see about my mail. It finally came. I got my haircut and had lunch. When we got back to the RV park in Surrey, we cleaned out all the bays in the motor coach. Maurice cooked some steaks on the grill outside and we had a wonderful meal. We needed time out.

Maurice fixed a wonderful breakfast the next morning, then we went to Vancouver, British Columbia, and to Stanley Park, which was terrific. Then we went into town and had lunch at Steam Works, a real nice place on the water. After lunch we went to Gastown to see the sites and the famous gas clock, which is very unusual. When we left Vancouver, we stopped by the grocery store and on to the RV park. Next day, we went on errands then left for Cache Creek, British Columbia. We spent the night at Cache Creek and did some catching up on the motor coach. The highway we covered that day was so beautiful. Everything is so clean. Maurice drove the whole way, for we were in and out of so many high places. We had dinner and just relaxed.

We left Cache Creek early and headed for Prince George. We arrived at 4 pm, and set up for the night.

We spent the next day in Denali Park. We took the six-hour bus trip and saw very little wildlife, but the scenery was very nice.

Coming back to the visitor center, a moose came out of the brush and started walking down the road in front of the bus. It finally went back into the brush.

We got off the bus early going back and went to the sled dog camp. That was very interesting. We saw all the sled dogs, took pictures, patted them, and had a mush demonstration. We got a book written by the manager of a sled dog team. The dog on the front of the book is named Sorrel, a very interesting book.

We left the next day for Fairbanks, Alaska. Alaska has only four major highways, #1,2, 3 and 4. We are staying at a nice park in Eielson Air Force Base by the lake, with a lot of Spruce trees. We got all set up and sat outside until it was time to eat.

We went into Fairbanks the next morning. Fairbanks is twenty-one miles south of where we are staying. We went to the visitor center, and got us certificates about travelling the Alaskan Hwy. We went to the Saturday Farmers Market and had a real nice time. We went back downtown and took the walking tour, which had a lot of history. We got back then went and checked out the emails in the office. A lot of very nice people from Texas were in the park.

We arrived at Smithers, British Columbia at the Glacier View RV Park. It is a very nice park facing the glacier. We went into town, did a little sightseeing, did some shopping. We then went to see the Twin Falls out in the countryside, which is simply beautiful.

We left Smithers, and headed for Steward, BC. We stopped several times on the road and took pictures, for the sights were so beautiful. Took a side trip into Old Hazelton. It was another interesting place. We had lunch at the Hummingbird Restaurant. The view was wonderful. We traveled to a place called Kitwanga at the Gitxsan Paintbrush. We did some Christmas shopping.

We stopped along the highway several times and saw a total of five bears, they were by the water streams or trash cans. We arrived at Steward early evening, relaxed the rest of the evening.

On June 15, we left early and drove and found the road was blocked with snow, went to Salman Glacier in Hyder, Alaska. It was awesome – we drove until we couldn't drive anymore for the road was blocked with snow. We stopped coming to Steward and had lunch in the car. We didn't want the bears to get a whiff of our food. Did some rock hunting, for I would love to start to paint rocks for a hobby (they also sell well). We stopped in the town of Hyder, but there was not much to see. It's called the friendliest ghost town in Alaska. Robin Williams made a film here, called Insomnia, in 2002.

Arrived back in Steward and looked around town, which took about ten minutes. We stopped and got an ice cream cone, then went back to the RV park. While we were in Hyder eating our ice cream there was an avalanche up above us. It was visible from the start high above and stopped in the canyon near Hyder. We were not expecting that. We watched Johnny Carson tapes when we got back to the coach.

On Father's Day, June 16, I took Maurice out to breakfast while he was having the coach washed. (did it need it). We left Stewart and drove as far as Dease, BC. The roads were 90% gravel and what a mess. The Honda we were towing got all rock chipped and front windshield cracked. Dust was everywhere. The motor coach looked like it had been through a dust storm, (so much for the wash job). I can say though the drive was so beautiful, and the sky so blue. We went out for dinner. When we got back, we cleaned some more. Dust, dust and more dust. We planned to leave in the morning for Whitehorse, Lord willing.

We left Dease Lake and arrived in Johnson's Crossing early evening. We stayed in a real nice RV Park. Mosquitos are a hazard, but other than that, everything turned out fine.

We left in the morning for Skagway and Whitehorse. The country here in the Yukon is so beautiful, lush with green everywhere.

We arrived in Skagway today, what a beautiful sight. I drove from Johnson's Crossing and had to go through a pass to get to Skagway, (that was an experience). We got set up in the RV park and went into town and saw a film on Skagway. Skagway is in a National Park. We did some sightseeing; Maurice took some pictures and did some more Christmas shopping. We planned to take a train ride the next day. We had dinner at Portabella, very nice place. Maurice went back to the Post Office to see about his mail again. His came, mine did not. I planned to call the next day about the status. We got up early and Maurice went to see about the tickets for the train ride, White Horse Pass. We got the 1:45 pm tour and enjoyed it so much. It had so much history on the tour. Earlier in the morning we got a lot of correspondence done and just relaxed.

We left Skagway and stopped in Carcross. It was a very old town on the water. There was a General Store, the oldest store operating in BC. We ate in a little building that was by the visitor center, sponsored by the Heritage Center. We arrived in Whitehorse, Yukon, and got set up and had a light dinner. We stayed at an RV park called Mackenzie, which was very nice.

We took it easy the next morning, then went into town for sightseeing. It's a very interesting town in the Yukon. The whole area of the Yukon is beautiful and so alive. The population is 35,000 for the whole Yukon but the land itself is 186,299 square miles. Made Maurice a King Ranch Chicken casserole and bread pudding. He said it was yummy.

We went touring Whitehorse, Yukon, and saw the USS Klondike. The USS Klondike (AD-22) was one of four destroyer tenders built at the tail end of World War II for the United States Navy. The lead ship in her class, she was named for the Klondike River in the Yukon Territory, Canada, was the scene of the gold rush of 1897. We also went to Miles Canyon and it was so beautiful. We went to the airplane museum and Ice Age Museum.

What a wonderful sight when we saw the sign, Welcome to Alaska, but the roads were horrible. Poor Maurice had to wash the RV and car. It was dusty everywhere. I cleaned all the windows inside and dusted everything down. I sure hoped the roads to Valdez are not that bad.

We left Tok early morning and headed for Valdez. The countryside was amazing on the way to Valdez. God's country is so wonderful, you think you had died and gone to heaven. We saw some of the most spectacular country. One thing was the Worthington Glacier and Thompson Pass. Well it's was raining that morning, so we just relaxed for a while. I did some emails; Maurice did some phone calling. We went for a long walk when the rain let up. I showed Maurice different places I went to when I was here in 99. We came back and had lunch then went out sightseeing. We also saw several films on Valdez, and how they survived the 1964 earthquake. The next morning, we packed a picnic lunch and went to Thompson Pass and took some pictures of Worthington Glacier. We walked toward the glacier, also read about the history of glaciers. We went to Keystone Canyon also took some pictures. Took pictures of Bridal Falls and Horsetail Falls. When we got back in Valdez, we went out to dinner at Pipeline Restaurant.

Maurice called his mother and wished her a happy birthday, then we left on the Prince Williams Sound day trip by boat. That was a great experience. We saw so much and met some real nice people. After getting back to Valdez, we went to a fish fry (good old salmon). We left this morning for Anchorage.

We arrived in Anchorage late. We were on a lot of narrow roads. We went to the Anchorage RV Park and they were filled. We then went to Elmendorf Air Force Base and got a place at the FAM Campground.

When we got set up, we went to the BX and commissary and did some shopping. I didn't mention I backed up the RV into our parking space for the first time. Hooray.

We got up early in the morning, and did a few things around the coach, then went to the air show at Elmendorf. The combined military forces presented a reenactment of the Pearl Harbor attack. It was unbelievable real and most interesting and educational. It was spectacular.

On June 20, observed longest day of year-21 hours sunlight.

June 30, 2002

Maurice and I had a leisurely morning, then we went to town and ran some errands. I got little upset at Walmart trying to get our pictures we had developed. Maurice got his, but mine were still not done. We also went to Costco and did some shopping. We had a great cook out that evening.

Chapter 9

July 2002

M aurice got up early and went and got the turn signals replaced on the Honda. We did some things around the RV that needed done. We went to the Native Alaskan Heritage Center. It was very educational, and we really enjoyed it. Maurice and I did some grocery shopping. I also got my haircut.

We took a day trip to Steward to see the Exist Glaciers. We had a wonderful lunch overlooking the lake. There was a large crowd coming in for the 4th of July. We came back to Hope, Alaska. A real old town.

There's not much to see, but very beautiful area. We went to the 4th of July parade in downtown Anchorage. We came back and ate lunch, and later went to a movie called "The Wind Talkers." We went out to dinner at Outback. Had a wonderful 4th, and thank you Lord, no terrorist.

Next day we went to Eagle Lake and Nature Center. We took a hike from the Center but didn't see any eagles there. Saturday, we took off to the Market Center. They have about anything you want. We did some Christmas shopping. When we got back home, we called our children. We made a point of calling each Saturday.

Sunday, Maurice and I went to church on base. After church we stayed in for a while for it looked like rain. We watched some movies. The weather cleared up and we went to the Anchorage Zoo. It was very nice. We saw a polar bear and a brown bear that the news had been talking about. We got back, fixed dinner, then drove up to Flat Top, which is a place to hike, a lovely place.

The next day we went to Homer on the Kenai Peninsula for the day. We had a nice time and had lunch at a restaurant that specializes in sourdough. We got back to Anchorage and dropped off some rental movies and stopped and ate at Burger King. Maurice and I ran some errands, made some phone calls, and shopped at the base. Maurice grilled some salmon on the grill. It was so, so good. I called Brenda twice, it's her birthday.

The next day we got ready to go to church on the base. After church we went into Fairbanks and visited the University of Alaska. The university is very interesting and date back to the Ice Age. We also took pictures of a Russian trade post that was part of the university.

July 15, 2002

Today Maurice and I stayed at the RV Park and worked on the coach. I baked some cookies and fixed dinner.

The next day we went to the base and did some shopping, did emails and some errands. We took a bike ride after dinner.

This morning Maurice and I went to the base again and did some more shopping, did some other errands, then we went on the Discovery Boat Ride down the Chena River. We got off the boat for an hour to go on an island and saw how the Athabasca Indians lived and survived some 10,000 years ago. After the boat ride, we went and got our mail. We got up on a nice morning and did more shopping. We went to Fairbanks and did some sightseeing, and got a book on rock painting, my new hobby.

Today we took a tour of Eielson AF Base. We covered the whole Base. We also went into the hangar where they do maintenance on the jet's they fly. It was a real interesting tour. After lunch we went into Fairbanks and got all the paint to do my rock painting. We also went to a movie called Road to Perdition. Later in the afternoon we went to Alaskasland.

We saw a lot of old houses and businesses that had been moved from downtown Fairbanks. After that we went to a flower show put on by the community.

The next day, we went to another parade. We love parades. This marked the Gold Rush Days in Alaska. The parade was so good, a little long. It was so cold, then raining. Sunday, we went to church then over to the Four Season's Club on base and ate lunch. We went for a bike ride and fed the ducks at the pond. We got back to the RV and started getting ready to leave in the morning for Tok. Later in the evening we went to see the movie, "The Ya-Ya Sisters" which was very enjoyable.

We arrived in Tok about 1:15 pm. We spent the night and traveled to Dawson City, Yukon, in the morning. We went to the post office and did some emailing later. Tok is a very small place, but interesting. The post office is kind of in the woods, but the bush mail plane lands right by the post office. I couldn't believe my eyes when it came in to pick up the mail. No landing area.

We left Tok, traveling to Dawson City. I'll never forget the roads are very narrow, real gravel all over, dust everywhere. Sometimes I felt like we were on two wheels, I never want to go back that way. On the other hand, we did get to the top of the world. Really, it was such a sensation. When we got parked, we went and saw some sights in Dawson City and ate at a real nice restaurant. Dawson City is a real old mining town. They still do mining there. It was a very interesting place. Only 144 miles from the Arctic Circle but it would take you about twelve hours to drive there. The roads are so rough.

We left the next morning for Whitehorse, Yukon. We couldn't find a good camping place, so we had to settle for a very undesirable place at Steward Crossings. We washed clothes and sent some emails, also did shopping.

We went to church in town. After church we went to get a Sunday paper and found out they don't have a Sunday paper in Whitehorse. It's rained all-night, went out to the RV park we had stayed at and did some emails, worked on some papers, we watched a movie that night, "Mulholland Fall."

While in Whitehorse we had a problem with the RV. A rock hit a fan blade and the radiator. A real nice gentleman from a repair shop let us stay there all week without charge, but Maurice paid him when we left. We had to order the parts from Junction City, Oregon, so that's when I started painting rocks.

The next morning, we went to Miles Canyon and took a walking tour. We saw an outlay of what Canyon City used to be like, which was one hundred years old. I woke up this morning feeling under the weather, so I stayed inside.

August 1, 2002

We waited for the coach to be finished this morning. I went and did some shopping, washed clothes and went to the post office. We ate lunch, then left for Watson Lake, Yukon. Spent the night at Watson Lake. Later we went to eat at the Belledov Hotel.

Maurice and I left Watson Lake and headed for Fort Nelson. We couldn't find any place to stay at Fort Nelson, so we traveled 70 miles until we got to Prophet River, a very small place. I must say that the day was blessed by seeing so many wildlife: moose, goats, horses and buffalo.

We left the little town of Prophet River, going to Dawson Creek. We arrived in Dawson Creek by early noon. We took the motor coach and washed it again. The road was a mess again. In the spring and summer, they are always working on the roads for that is the only time they have before the weather sets in. We saw some beautiful country on the way to Dawson Creek. We set up camp and checked our email. We rested a while, then went to the visitor center and got some information. We looked around town, took pictures and went shopping. Later we went out to eat dinner at Mr. Mikes. We had a very enjoyable evening. I think that today was one of the most beautiful drives we have had, but I may be repeating myself. The weather was cool (38), snow on the mountains, the scenery was awesome.

What beautiful country we've seen today. British Columbia is so amazing. It's amazing how God has placed everything in its place. I started out driving. After about two hours, a deer ran out in front of the coach. I don't know whose heart was beating the fastest, the deer or mine. We almost had veal cutlets for dinner. As we traveled on down the highway, I believe that I have seen enough sewer hoses from RVs to pave a small highway. After we had lunch on the road Maurice took over the driving. We saw a herd of buffalo, a group of rock sheep and a moose run right out in front of the coach. Well, we missed another chance, moose cutlets. We arrived in Jasper, BC at 6 pm, staying at the Whistlers Provincial campgrounds.

It's like a national park we have in the states, but so big. I've never seen anything quite like it. Brenda and John were to meet with us the next day. We planned to stay for about five nights, then go to Banff, BC.

We moved into a campsite this morning with hook-up. We had to dry camp last night. It got down to almost freezing. We had to go to the entrance gate and wait until someone moved out of a space. Thank goodness he was the first to arrive. Later in the day, we went into the town of Jasper and did some sightseeing. It's very neat little town. It reminds me of a ski resort.

Today was kind of special. We went outside and just relaxed, watched the birds, squirrels and had a large deer come almost into our camp space. We went into town and checked our email, then went to the post office. We came back to the RV Park, had lunch and relaxed some more. Brenda and John arrived about 2 pm. They also had to dry camp overnight. We visited for a while and later went back into town with Brenda and John for dinner. We had Chinese food. After dinner we drove over to Pyramid Lake and looked it over. It was so beautiful. It had a little island that you walked over to. It also had a beautiful lodge there. We really enjoyed having Brenda and John visiting in the same park.

We got up next morning and did a few things around the coach, then went with Brenda and John to Athabasca Falls, Angel Glacier, Mount Edith Cavell and Lake Edith, also Sunwapta Falls. Everything we saw was so breathtaking. At the Mount Edith Cavell we went on a forty-minute hike. We arrived back in town of Jasper and went to the Karroo's Restaurant. We got back to the coach and just relaxed and visited with Brenda and John.

We got up the next morning. The four of us took a trip to Medicine Lake, which was so beautiful. The Indians believed the water that disappears each year was to do with the Medicine Man, but the water is going into Maligne Canyon area. We also went to the Maligne Lake, which is the largest lake in Jasper National Park. Maligne Canyon has six different foot bridges, which have a spectacular view.

When we got back to town, we stopped at the grocery store to get something to grill outside, which Maurice did.

The next day Brenda and I had a nice day being together, sister time. We went to the Miette Hot Springs and then out to lunch. We returned to Jasper downtown area and did some shopping. The springs were so relaxing (my first). Brenda and John had us over for dinner and of course John put on a feast.

The next morning, we got up and the four of us went hiking. We went back to Maligne Lake and covered the fifth and sixth bridges. We also covered the fourth bridge again. After we were through, we had a picnic then went into Jasper and did some email and grocery shopping. Maurice and I went over to Brenda and Johns and ate dinner again with them.

I guess I never wrote that when we started RVing, Maurice got a forty-foot motor home and a Honda Accord tow car. We traveled for about four years, then bought a forty-five foot because we loved it so much. During the time we first met, Maurice sold a house and then a condo. RVing is a great lifestyle.

The next day we had Brenda and John over for brunch, afterwards we just relaxed. Later that afternoon, we all went bike riding around the RV Park. Brenda came over later and got me to take some pictures of the elk that was by their coach. There were four females and four baby Elk. They were very calm.

Today we left Jasper for Banff. We stopped by the Columbia Icefields and it was so amazing. We rode out on the glaciers on a large bus with tires that were about the height of our car. We took a lot of pictures of all the surroundings. The four of us went back to the center and had lunch.

We said our goodbyes and Brenda and John went on to Golden, then back to the states. Maurice and I arrived in Banff about 4 pm, set up the coach and went to get our mail. We also checked on where we could email and looked around the area. After breakfast, Maurice and I had a very enjoyable day. We went for a hike around the Banff Springs Hotel, which looks like a castle. The hotel was built back in the early 1900s by the railroad company (Canadian Pacific). They used the material to build the hotel from the area of Banff.

We had a wonderful buffet lunch at the hotel, which had any and everything, it was a feast to say the least. I believe we both overdid it. Later that afternoon we went sightseeing and took some more pictures.

We got up early, had a good breakfast and went into Banff and went to the post office. It looked like rain, so we stayed around downtown. It started pouring, so we went into several shops. We stayed in one shop and did some shopping for the grandchildren. When we got back to the coach, we prepared the items we got for mailing. We took it easy the rest of the day for it continued to rain.

Maurice and I went to Johnson Canyon and took a hike up to the highest falls. They have a lower fall and a higher fall. Both were so beautiful. On the way back down, I took a terrible fall and really thought I was going over the edge of the cliff. Maurice caught me as I was rolling over toward the cliff, thank God.

Earlier in the morning we went to the post office, sent emails and I called Morgan, my grandson, for it's his birthday (20) years, hard to believe.

Today we went to Lake Louise, also the Chateau. The lake was named after Queen Victoria's daughter (Louise). The lake is such a beautiful emerald green and a glacier is right behind it. We made reservations for Sunday brunch after church. We also went to Lake Moraines. We went to see Takkakaw Falls, the largest in Canada. A film company from India was making a film at the Falls. We had a very enjoyable day. We also saw large glacier named Yoho Glacier near Takkakaw.

We stayed around Banff today and ran some errands, then went to Canada Place (downtown Banff), which shows some history about Canada. There was a beautiful flower garden with a lot of Burly Wood, which is common in the areas. After we left Canada Place, we went to the Cave and Basin, which was discovered by three young gentleman in the 1800s by accident. It was a very interesting place, and at one time a very popular place to go. On the way back to the RV Park, we stopped and saw some rock formations called the Hoodoos.

August 18, Maurice and I left early and went to Lake Louise. First, we rode the Gondola, which was so nice, such an experience. I really enjoyed it. Maurice is so much fun to be with. We then went to Chateau Lake Louise and had Sunday Brunch. On the way back to Banff we saw a lot of cars parked on the side of the road. We stopped. There were two black bears eating berries. Of course, I had to take some pictures. We returned to the RV park and started getting ready to leave the next morning for Calgary.

We left Banff for Calgary he next day, arrived around 11 am, set up in camp, and went to see about our mail, which we received. We then went to the grocery store and relaxed for the evening.

We got the oil changed in the Honda. While they changed the oil in the coach also, we went to a movie "Bloodwork" which was very interesting, with Clint Eastwood who always plays a great part. We ran a few errands and retired for the evening.

After breakfast, Maurice and I went into Calgary downtown, to do some sightseeing. Calgary is the fastest growing city in Canada. It's very modern city. We did some shopping at Hudson Bay (founded in 1600s) and ate lunch there also.

We left this morning for Winnipeg. We traveled all day and spent the night dry camping in a church parking lot. We felt very blessed. We arrived in Winnipeg area and set up camp at an RV park in Portage, about thirty-eight miles west of Winnipeg. It was a nice park, but the water was terrible. We went into Winnipeg to sightsee. We took a boat ride at the Fork on the Red River. Winnipeg is a very interesting city. We did some shopping and went to the Air Force Base, but no luck, very small.

Today Maurice and I left early and went back to Winnipeg and did some more sightseeing. We went to a very old church that was built elsewhere in 1818, and later moved its congregation to a new location. That church burn, the front frame of the church still stands but they have built a new church inside the old. It's unique. We visited the museum of the Grey Nuns, real interesting. We had lunch at the Falls on the water at Muddy Slide. We also went to Fort Garry Hotel, which is very historical, also the Legislative Building and the gardens.

Chapter 10

O n the road again (as Willie would say) to Ontario. We stayed at a Park on Crystal Lake in Vermillion, (the owners are strange). We did some things around the coach. Maurice grilled some salmon for dinner, and we watched the movie on TV, "Godfather II."

We stayed another night in Vermillion. Maurice and I went into town and mailed some post cards and looked around. It's a very small town, mainly a fishing town. The next morning, we left Vermillion on the way to Schreiber, Ontario. We drove all day, spent the night and left in the morning for Sault Ste Marie.

We got up and got ready to leave for Sault Ste. Marie. We arrived about 4pm, staying at a nice RV Park right off Hwy 17. It's also a town that crossed over to the good ole USA, Michigan. We went to the boardwalk in Sault Ste. Marie and saw several people fishing and saw them catch some beautiful salmon. Maurice and I had dinner in town and returned to do some emails. Today we are leaving for Sudbury and staying at Carol's Campsite by Richard Lake. It's a large park, we met some real nice neighbors next to us from Calgary. We set up and went into downtown to get our mail, then just looked around. Maurice grilled outside and later we took a walk down to the lake.

September 1, 2002

Maurice and I went on a picnic and looked around Sudbury. We went to Ramsey Lake today and walked around the boardwalk. Ramsey Lake is a very large lake not too far from downtown Sudbury. We fed the seagulls some bread that I had saved. Later we got some movies from Blockbuster, then did some shopping.

On Labor Day, we ran a few errands, the checked our emails. We got everything ready for our trip to Toronto tomorrow. We wanted to leave early. We have some new neighbors today. They are from Lake Livingston, Texas. We had a long visit with them, and just relaxed the rest of the day. We got up and left around 7:30 am for Toronto. We stayed and got the car repaired, then on to Cornwall.

Today, September 4, is Maurice and my anniversary for meeting a year ago on the plane, (that I almost missed). It's been such a blessing. We went to Niagara Falls, and it was awesome. We took so many pictures, and rode on the boat, Maid of the Mist. That was an experience. Then we had lunch at the Hard Rock Cafe. After lunch we walked around the waterfront. It was a perfect day. Thank you so much Lord.

Another beautiful day, Maurice and I planned to go into Toronto City. We went on a tour of the Casa Loma Castle. It was so beautiful and very interesting. It truly had a lot of good history, but heartache too. After the tour we went to downtown Toronto and that was a mistake. Toronto has over two million people, and I was almost convinced they were all there downtown. On the way back to RV park, we did some errands and went by a farmer's house to get some real nice fresh vegetables and fruit.

This morning we left for Cornwall, arrived about 3pm. We got all set up and went to see about the battery for the coach and windshield in the car, also the car lights. I went and got our mail at the post office. Maurice's mail didn't arrive yet but should be here Monday. We went grocery shopping, got back and did some things around the coach and just relaxed.

Maurice and I are going on a picnic and look around Sudbury. We went to Ramsey Lake today and walked around the boardwalk. Ramsey Lake is a very large Lake not too far from downtown Sudbury. We fed the Sea Gulls some bread that I had saved. Later we went and got some movies from Blockbuster, then did some shopping.

Today September 7th, Maurice's birthday. I fixed breakfast for him, then we went for a bike ride, ran some errands, went to 5 pm church. I took him to dinner at a Mexican restaurant. He was really surprised.

Monday September 8th, we planned to go to a classic car show. They had all kinds of makes and models. We also saw a Hydro boat race and looked over several islands outside of Cornwall, a very relaxing day.

This morning we took a bike ride. It was very refreshing it's so warm here. We went on a walking tour of the Lost Villages (6), that were flooded or moved because of the flood plain. The buildings that were moved were done well.

Today is my middle daughter's birthday. I talked with her and she sounded in good spirits. Maurice got the battery for the coach replaced, got the lights replaced on the Honda, ran several errands and sent each one of our children letters and pictures. Maurice and I went out to dinner. When we got back, we started getting ready to leave in the morning for Quebec City.

We arrived in Quebec in the rain. It rained all day and night. We had to change parking places for the electricity wouldn't work. We finally got settled for the evening. We planned to go into Quebec City in the morning.

We left about 7:30 am this morning to catch the Grey Line bus into Quebec City for a tour. It was so wonderful, so full of history. We went into a church that was established in the 16th century. After the tour, we took the bus to Portofino Restaurant for lunch, it was quite French. After lunch we walked and shopped, and saw the sights, until it was time to go back to the bus terminal. We must have walked miles.

We left Quebec at 8:40am this morning and stopped in a campground not far from New Brunswick called Causapscal. We got all setup, took a brief walk then fixed dinner. After dinner I wrote some post cards.

September 14 is a traveling day. We arrived at Caraquet, N.B. for the night. Maurice and I got up to leave and it was raining so hard we stayed another day. Rain, rain and more rain. We got out and went grocery shopping. Came back to camp and stayed inside.

The next day the rain had gone. We traveled to Shediac and arrived about 2 pm. It is beautiful. We settled into a nice RV Park by the water, the sail boats are everywhere.

We were on the inland of the Atlantic Ocean. Lobster is famous in Shediac. We went to a drive thru and got fresh steamed lobster. What a treat for dinner.

This morning, we drove over to Prince Edward Island from Shediac. The island is simply beautiful, rolling hills, farmland and so many different types of houses and churches. We saw a cruise ship docked by a restaurant.

After lunch we took a walk around the shops and government buildings. We planned to go back Saturday for the seafood feast.

We got up this morning and drove over to Moncton, N.B., to visit the Atlantic Baptist Heritage, which was so interesting, a nice gentleman explained things to us and gave us meal tickets for us to have lunch with him in the lunchroom. After lunch we left and went shopping and did some sightseeing. It was another beautiful day, going to Sussex, N.B., to get our mail. Maurice got his, I didn't. Oh well – On the way to Sussex we dropped off some film at Walmart and picked them up on the way back to the campground. We also had lunch at Sussex. Sussex is a very old town. We didn't do much sightseeing. We planned to go back in about a week.

We got up early the next morning and went back to Prince Edward Island. We covered a large area of Prince Edward Island, which included Summerside, an area that use to be a big Silver Fax industry. We took a car tour of old homes. The homes were real pretty with a lot of different architecture. On the way to the North Cape, we stopped and took pictures of the Moss Horses, which the people use to rake seaweed from shallow water and on the beaches. Certain parts of seaweed are sold for making different ingredient for food products, make-up, also ice cream.

We arrived at the North Cape in Prince Edward Island, which is the farthest Point north. We had lunch at a very nice restaurant. After lunch we went walking on the beach. We left there and went to Green Gables to see where LM Montgomery lived when she was a child. She wrote the book "Anne of Green Gables". We went on the tour of the house, barn and walked down Lover's Lane, and other trails. The grounds were so beautiful there at Green Gables. After that we traveled on to Charlottes Town for the Shellfish Festival, which was very interesting. We watched the entertainment for a while, a band from Nova Scotia. For dinner, we went to a nice Mediterranean style restaurant. We got back at the RV park in Shediac, a very full day, but a great one.

We left Shediac the next day and traveled to Nova Scotia. We are planning to see the Cabot Trails tomorrow. We settled in a waterfront RV park and the scenery is beautiful. Maurice and I plan to be here about three days.

The scenery we saw at Breton Island, N.S. was simply magnificence. I don't believe I have experienced anything so beautiful. It took all day to drive the Cabot Trails, which was discovered by Capt. Cabot in 1497. The island is full of Celtic arts and crafts. We also traveled some back roads, which was very interesting. Cape Breton Highlands National Park is in the Cabot Trails, where there are pull outs, so you can take a lot of beautiful pictures. We ate at the Crowder House at Neil's Harbor, which was recommended by Brenda and John. The food was very good, especially the Clam Crowder. You don't hurt for seafood here in Nova Scotia area. We plan to drive the Sunrise area tomorrow, which is the upper north part of Nova Scotia, not too far from the RV Park we are in. Well it rained today. We drove over to Cape George, Sunrise Trail. We also went to a Creamy to see about tickets for a Celtic Musical. Celtic means "Music in the Kitchen". We really enjoyed the young people that were playing instruments and dancing.

September 25, Maurice and I drove from Monastery to Nine Miles River, Peggy's Cove. Peggy's Cove was so beautiful with a very charming lighthouse. We bought some post cards and sat down on the rocks around the lighthouse and wrote them to our children. We also sent them from the lighthouse. We saw a lot of sail boats, and walked around the village, a beautiful little fishing village, went to the monument for the Swiss air crash back in the 90s. We drove along the shores of more fishing villages.

We took another day trip and covered a lot of ground. We went to Windsor, saw several house Museums (Halliburton and Shand) and both were very interesting. We also went to Grand Pyre to the Evangeline Museum, about the Acadian people. We ate at a local restaurant called the Evangeline Inn. Going back to the RV park, we went through Wolfville, N.S. where Acadia University is.

Chapter 11

•••••••

Today we left for Fundy National Park. We stopped off at Springfield in Nova Scotia, at the Anne Murray Center and took the tour which was very nice. Springfield is Anne Murray's hometown. Maurice bought me a T-shirt from the gift shop. We arrived at the Fundy National Park, and it started raining, so we set up for camp, then went into Sussex, N.B. and picked up our mail and did some grocery shopping. Judy, my cousin, had brain surgery today.

Maurice and I drove into the Alma post office today, then rode around the countryside. We went hiking in the National Park by the seashore. We saw Dickson Fall, Herron Cove, and picked up rocks for our collection. Morning came, and we left early to see the Cape Enrage Lighthouse. It was so enchanting way up high on a point, such a wonderful place. The students in the area keep up the grounds. We then went to Hopewell Rock, saw the low tide and walked on the ocean floor. The displacement of the tides in this area is huge. We went onto Hopewell Rock to see the high tides, went into Moncton to do some shopping, then went back to Hopewell Rock to see the high tides. (One of God's wonders).

Maurice and I went into Alma to check the tides on Fundy Bay the next morning. We did some email at an old school, had dinner at the "Tides" in Alma on the water in Fundy Bay. We saw a film at Fundy National Park. Later that evening talked with Annie my cousin about her sister Judy that had brain surgery, she said was doing well.

We went down to Alma and walked on the ocean floor, also searched for rocks. Then rode around Fundy and took some hiking trails, then went back to the RV park. Maurice cooked out. As always, it was great. Prepared to leave for St. John's area tomorrow.

We arrived in Pocologan, N.B. around 11:15 am and met a nice couple in the RV park from Kansas, John and Peggy. Maurice and I visited with them for a while and just relaxed for the rest of the day.

The next day Maurice and I went into St. John's and took a tour of the city. We had lunch at Don Cherry's restaurant, which very good. The dessert was awesome. The tour was very interesting, the narrator did a wonderful job, we saw a lot of history. Maurice and I also went to the famous City Market, but I wasn't impressed, I was very disappointed, so was Maurice. After the tour, we did some shopping and ran some errands. The next day we did some things around the coach, then went for a road tour on our own. We drove to the ferry that goes to Deer Island and had a real nice ferry ride, next to St. George, Beaver Code, Black Harbor, all on the Fundy Bay area. We had dinner at a little seafood restaurant. The weather got bad during the night and continued through the day, so we stayed in. Maurice did paperwork; I worked on the photo book.

The next day we rode over to Fredericton just northeast of here. We took the back roads and the foliage was very beautiful. The countryside going and coming back was just breathtaking. We ate lunch in Fredericton and made some phone calls, for the cell phone worked better there. When we got back to the RV park, we prepared to leave in the morning for Ellsworth, Maine.

Chapter 12

• • ● • •

October 7, well we are back in the good ole USA. What a welcoming site, mainly for what is going on in the world. I pray we will have peace very soon. Maurice and I have had a wonderful trip so far, such a wonderful relationship. We arrived at the RV park around 11 am, set up, ate lunch then went to Bangor to get our mail. I also got a haircut, which I really needed. We went grocery shopping, also to another store and got some more photo books.

We got up early this morning and went to Bar Harbor, Maine. The area is very old on the coast. It's very beautiful, with a lot of tourists. We saw the Carnival Legend Cruise ship. We walked along the shoreline, which was so refreshing, so much to see and do there. We also went to the Acadia National Park, which is simply beautiful. It's a twenty-seven-mile drive around the whole park. We ate lunch at the Jordan restaurant in the park, overlooking the Jordan Lake. When we returned to Ellsworth, we ran some errands and got our film developed. Later that evening we prepared to leave in the morning for Vermont.

We left Ellsworth, Maine this morning. Maurice and I went by the post office in Bangor to pick up some more mail. We stayed at a visitor center in New Hampshire and ate lunch in the coach. We got turned around several times today but managed to get to the RV park. We were tired puppies when we retired tonight.

The next morning, we drove around the loop in Vermont to see the foliage. We found some pretty nice areas, but really feel the foliage had already peaked. Vermont is such a lovely place. We stopped and ate at an old family restaurant that was very good. We continued our drive. We stopped in Manchester for about an hour and did some shopping. It started raining, so we knew we were through taking pictures for the day. The drive was so nice through the countryside, we returned to the RV park, had dinner and prepared to leave the next day.

We arrived in Hershey, Pa. around 10 am, found the Chocolate World and took the tour of history of the founder and the factory. We also saw a 3-D of the Hershey Chocolate Company. We left Hershey and went to Lancaster, Pa. We stayed at a campground overlooking an Amish farm.

This morning we went sightseeing and had a relaxing day. We went out to eat at Friendly's Restaurant – family style.

Today we went to church at 11:30 am, rode through the countryside. The countryside is so lovely. After church we went to Intercourse, Pa. but everything was closed. We found the Amish Barn restaurant in another little town they also had a gift shop, so we enjoyed looking and shopping there. When we got back to the RV park, we went to the Amish Village they have in the park. We saw a film on the history of the Amish. Later in the evening, we watched a Jackie Gleason movie.

On Columbus Day (October 14), we went back to Intercourse, Pa. For everything was closed on Sunday. We went into several shops at the Amish Village. We also rode a lot in the Amish countryside. We went to the Toy Train museum. It was very interesting. We got back to the RV park and prepared to leave for Virginia in the morning.

We left Lancaster this morning for Virginia. We sure had a nice time in Lancaster area. We arrived at the Quantico Base campground, set up and then went to the post office to get Maurice's mail, then we went to the Base PX.

Maurice and I went to Washington, DC to sightsee. It was pouring down rain, but we managed to get where we wanted to go. We went to several museums and had lunch at the Museum of History. We had a very nice time, only problem, was we got caught in the 4pm traffic, it took us two hours to get back to the RV park, normally took forty-five minutes to drive.

Today we did some things around the motor coach, ran some errands, later we went over to Susie and Jan's house. I worked with Susie when I lived in Virginia. We had a real nice visit, and when Jan got home, the four of us went out to eat dinner at a family Italian restaurant. After dinner we had Susie and Jan come out to the RV park and see the motor coach. They were very impressed. Jan wanted to go right out and buy one. We really had a nice evening with them.

Maurice and I got up early and went back into Washington, DC to the Vietnam Memorial and Air and Space Museum. We also saw two I-Max films which were very good, both by Lockheed Martin.

We got up early and left to see about Maurice's mail and go by the Base Exchange. Then I went over to Susie's to visit for a while. Her mother and dad had come in from Ohio, so we visited a while. I hadn't seen her mom since '91. When I got back to the RV park, Maurice had washed the motor coach and it shined, shined, shined. He changed his clothes and we went to the base commissary. When we got back, we had a couple from Quebec with two little boys staying by us. They were so cute; we sure miss our own grandchildren. We put the groceries up. Maurice made a fire outside. The couple came over and we sat outside for a while. We really enjoyed their company. They were headed for Florida for six months. We ate dinner and started getting ready to leave in the morning for Savannah.

We were on the road at 8:30 am, and had heard there had been another shooting, by the east coast sniper, that makes twelve. I prayed to God the snipers will soon be caught here in Virginia.

We made it to Florence, SC, and parked in the Walmart parking lot for the night. Maurice and I ate at the Red Lobster, which was very good. We planned to leave for Savannah in the morning.

We arrived in Savannah and found out the RV park was not what we expected, so we unhitched the car and went to several parks. We finally settled at the State Park. We got settled and ran some errands and made phone calls. The next morning, we went to Sam's Wholesale and Sharon (my sister) met us there.

Sharon and I left Maurice at Sam's and went into town to do some sightseeing, then to River Street. After lunch we walked along the riverfront. We ran a few errands, then went back to the RV park and visited for a while. Maurice grilled outside for the two of us for dinner.

Today we went to Tybee Beach. It was so nice to be on the beach and walk and find seashells. It was a little cool though. We also went by to see Tom (my cousin) at the golf course.

We bought some things for Christmas gifts. We did some more shopping, then went back to the RV park. We had Sharon and her family over for dinner.

Maurice and I ran a lot of errands today (October 24). We tried to locate an internet connection, but no luck. We had lunch at the famous "Mrs. Wilkes Boarding House". That was delightful treat. We both enjoyed it. We went to a musical at the Historical Savannah Theater to see "Lost in the 50s". It was a great musical, very funny.

Today we stayed home, caught up on writing notes, making phone calls and sending pictures to the family.

We got up this morning and just stayed around the coach. We went to 5:30 pm church services at St. John the Baptist. We later went to Wilmington Island for Paul's (my cousin) birthday party. They had seventy-two people at the party. They had a great band. It was also wonderful time. Maurice and I sat at the table with Paul and Judy. Judy looked great after her brain surgery.

We got up and had breakfast and went for a bike ride. We tried to go for a nature walk, but the mosquitoes were terrible. We went to the Byrd Cookie Company. It was really a treat eating all the samples of cookies. We met with Sharon and Denny at the Antique Show downtown at the Civic Center. After leaving there we went to the Piccadilly Café to eat.

We left for Jacksonville the next morning. We stayed at the Flamingo Lake RV Park. We got set up then went over to my other sister's house. We visited for a while, then went and had lunch at a nice place called Charley's. Sandra and Junior came out to see the motor coach, then we went to dinner on the waterfront in downtown Jacksonville. Junior (my brother-in-law) made a couple of CD's for Maurice, which he really enjoyed.

The next day we went over to Sandra and Junior's and went to the beach. We walked on the beach, in the water and found a lot of seashells. We then went to eat lunch.

After lunch we went to St. Augustine and walked around the Colonial Village. We also went to the RV park Sandra and Junior go to each summer. It was a great day out. We had a wonderful visit with Sandra and Junior.

Next day we left Jacksonville to see my brother and his wife in Palatka, Florida. It was so good to see them. Maurice really enjoyed meeting Sue and Dennis. Next day Dennis fixed a wonderful meal and had his son and family out, real good fellowship.

October 31, Halloween. Sue fixed breakfast and it was so good. They really know how to feed you. Maurice and I ran some errands, Sue had to get ready for a horseshow for the weekend, Dennis had a report to do for work. While we were out, we went back to St. Augustine to an Outlet Mall. Later we went back to Dennis's, visited a while and Dennis fixed dinner again. Boy can he cook. We offered to take them to dinner, but they wanted to stay at home. We retired early, for Dennis and Sue had to get ready to leave town for the weekend.

Chapter 13

November 1

Maurice and I prepared the coach to leave for New Orleans. Sue fixed another wonderful breakfast. We drove to Milton, Florida, just east of Pensacola, Florida and stayed at a KOA Park, very nice. We got set up then went to Navarre Beach about twenty miles south of the RV Park. The sunset was beautiful. We walked along the beach, then went to dinner at a nice seafood restaurant.

We left for New Orleans. We arrived in New Orleans at a most undesirable RV park, but it was close to everything. We then went to visit some of Maurice's in laws, Joy and Joe, (his sister-in-law and brother-in-law), then had a nice dinner in town. We left there and went over to the Riverwalk that has over 149 shops.

Maurice and I got up early and left for Houston. It rained the whole day on us. We saw a fifth wheel turned over. It sure makes you feel funny but thank the Lord we haven't seen that many accidents in travel trailers. We got to Houston around 5pm. I had already called and spoken with my children about meeting for dinner. My oldest daughter came and picked us up, and we all met at a nice Mexican restaurant. It was so wonderful to see my children and grandchildren. I really missed them. We got a ride back to the RV park and visited for a while. Maurice and I retired for the evening. We are leaving for Horseshoe Bay, Texas, in the morning.

We arrived in Marble Falls and parked at an RV park on the water. We made a few phone calls, then went to get the car inspected which was past due. They wouldn't inspected for it was raining. We really were disappointed. Later we went back to Maurice's daughter's for dinner. We really had a nice dinner and fellowship. It was so good to see everyone.

Maurice's granddaughters have grown so much. We took them one of their favorite desserts, a chocolate crème pie.

We got up early, had breakfast and went to get the car inspected. We took the bikes over to Maurice's house in Horseshoe Bay, got our flu shots and took the bike rack off the car and put it in his daughter's storage.

We got back to the coach and did a few chores. Maurice went to see about his elbow, which he had injured. He also went to vote, which I couldn't for I was in the wrong district.

November 6, 2002, we left Marble Falls this morning for Mexia to see Maurice's mother. She was sure glad to see us. We sat and visited for a while, then we went and got lunch for the three of us. She looked well and was doing good. We visited some more and left about 2:30 pm to go to Fort Worth.

We arrived in Fort Worth early evening and went to the RV park we left from on May 5. We have now made a complete circle. So many towns, so many cities, so many states and so many provinces. This trip has been a wonderful experience, which I will always cherish.

THE END.

THE FOLLOWING ARE PICTURES FROM OUR
TRIP. WE HOPE YOU ENJOY THEM.

COUNTRYSIDE
IN AKASKA

ALASKA BOTANICAL
GARDEN IN ANCHORAGE

HERE'S OUR CONDO
ON WHEELS

HOMER
ALASKA

PENISULA
HIGHWAY

COOPER'S
LANDING IN
ANCHORAGE

MOUNT
MC KINLEY

SLED DOG
MUCHING

SORRELL, ON
COVER OF BOOK
ABOUT SLEIGH DOGS

STATUE OF FIRST
FAMILY OF
FAIRBANKS

CAMPGROUND
IN FAIRBANKK
ALASKA

GARDENS AT THE
ALASKA
UNIVERSITY

RUSSIAN TRADING

POST AT UNIVERSITY

REINDEER ON AN
ISLAND WE VISITED

DISCOVERY III WE
RODE ON

JACKET MADE BY
AN ALASKAN INDIAN
WOMAN

REINDEER

LADY OF THE LAKE
WHERE THEY BURY

THEIR OLD AIRCRAFT
AT EIELSON AIR FORCE
BASE

IN THE PARADE IN ALASKA

ON OUR TRIP TO
THE TOP OF THE
WORLD

TOP OF THE WORLD

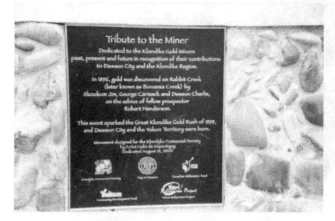

SIGNPOST FROM ALL
OVER THE WORLD

DAWSON CREEK

DAWSON CREEK

DOWNTOWN JASPER

MALIGNE LAKE

MALIGNE LAKE

DOWN IN THE VALLEY
OF GLACIER ANGEL IN
JASPER NAT'L PARK

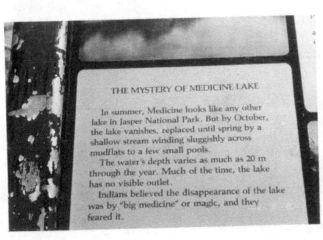

THE MYSTERY OF MEDICINE LAKE

In summer, Medicine looks like any other lake in Jasper National Park. But by October, the lake vanishes, replaced until spring by a shallow stream winding sluggishly across mudflats to a few small pools.

The water's depth varies as much as 20 m through the year. Much of the time, the lake has no visible outlet.

Indians believed the disappearance of the lake was by "big medicine" or magic, and they feared it.

MEDICINE LAKE

ICE ANGEL IN COLUMBIA
ICE FIELDS

BANFF SPRINGS HOTEL

DOWNTOWN BANFF

CHATEAU AT LAKE
LOUISE

HOODOO ROCK
FORMATIONS

LEGISLATIVE BLDG. IN
WINNIPEG

LAKE SUPERIOR ACROSS
FROM SAUTE STE MARIE

SALMON CAUGHT AT
SAUTE STE MARIE

FLOWER GARDEN IN
SUDBURY

NIAGARA FALLS

NIAGARA FALLS

NIAGARA FALLS
ROYAL AIR FORCE

98

HARD ROCK CAFÉ
IN TORANTO

CASA LOMA CASTLE IN
TORANTO

CASA LOMA CASTLE

MAURICE BIRTHDAY
IN CANADA

THE LOST VILLAGES

MURAL ON A BUILDING
IN QUEBEC

CHURCH IN QUEBEC CITY

OLDEST STREET IN

QUEBEC CITY

MURAL IN QUEBEC CITY

FURNICULAR IN

DOWNTOWN QUEBEC
CITY

RV PARK IN SHEDIAC

MOSS HORSES

NORTH CAPE

AUTHOR'S HOME

L.M. MONTGOMERY

AUTHOR OF GREEN

GABLES

BRETON ISLAND, NS
CABOT TRAILS

COASTAL AREA OF
BRETON ISLAND

FISHING VILLAGE AT
PEGGY'S COVE

NOVA SCOTIA

IN MEMORY OF
THE 229 MEN, WOMEN AND CHILDREN
ABOARD SWISSAIR FLIGHT III
WHO PERISHED OFF THESE SHORES
SEPTEMBER 2, 1998

THEY HAVE BEEN JOINED TO THE
SEA AND THE SKY

MAY THEY REST IN PEACE

CELTIC DANCERS AT
THE CREAMY

PEGGY'S COVE

IN GRATEFUL RECOGNITION OF
ALL THOSE WHO WORKED TIRELESSLY
TO PROVIDE ASSISTANCE IN THE RECOVERY
OPERATIONS AND COMFORT TO THE FAMILIES
AND THEIR FRIENDS DURING A TIME OF DISTRESS

ACADIAN PEOPLES
CHURCH

HALLIBURTON
MUSEUM IN NOVA
SCOTIA

SHORES OF FUNDY BAY

LIGHTHOUSE AT
CAPE ENAGE ON
FUNDY BAY

HOPEWELL ON
FUNDY BAY

DEER ISLAND IN
NEW BRUNSWICK

113

BAR HARBOR, MAINE

ACDIA NATIONAL

PARK

FOILAGE IN VERMON'

AMISH VILLAGE IN
PENN.

AMISH COUNTRYSIDE

CHOCOLATE WORLD

HERSHEY, PA.

THE MALL IN
WASHINGTON, DC

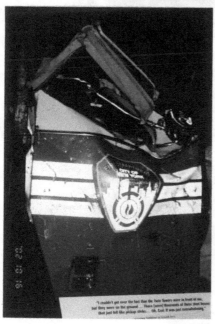

A DOOR FROM A FIRE
TRUCK FROM 911 AT
AMERICAN HISTORY
MUSEUM

FISHING PIER IN THE
PANHANDLE OF FLORIDA

OUR CONDO IN FLORIDA

LIGHTHOUSE IN
ST. AUGUSTINE, FL.

AT MY COUSIN'S
BIRTHDAY IN SAVANNAH

CPSIA information can be obtained
at www.ICGtesting.com
Printed in the USA
BVHW040148280620
582243BV00007B/77

9 781728 360355